WEALTH WARNING:

DON'T LET YOUR BOSS SEE YOU READING THIS!

You might like to remove the title page of this guide, if you don't want other people to see what you are studying. On the other hand it could be a tactic to leave it lying around (perhaps not a subtle one).

IMPORTANT DISCLAIMER

ABOUT THE AUTHOR

A fellow of the Chartered Institute of Bankers, A fellow of The Chartered Institute of Management. A business practitioner of Neuro Linguistic Programming and a member of the Institute of Directors.

Derek Arden started his career with Barclays and rose to be Director of Large Corporate Banking working in both Corporate and Investment Banking.

During his time at Barclays he worked in Management Development several times over a 10-year period, helping people maximise their talent.

He has taught negotiation skills for over 15 years notably at the Henley Management College but also at 4 other business schools and in 21 countries.

The largest negotiation that he was involved in was a hostile takeover where the total financing was in excess of £3bn.

As an author, teacher and coach Derek has been involved with advising, directing and coaching negotiations over a number of years.

He privately coaches people on all types of negotiating skills including salary and fees.

What people have said about Derek

"Without Derek's coaching I would not have had the nerve to have followed through on the negotiations which enabled me to increase my salary by £8000"

"The clear structure of the preparation and tactics made me conclude a very satisfactory situation - pay rise £10000"

"As a university graduate I managed to negotiate an extra £1000 into my Salary package with Derek's advice"

" My exit package was enhanced by £12000 as a result of Derek's direct help"

FOREWORD

Foreword by David Jones CBE
Chairman of UK retailer NEXT

David Jones is one of the most admired men in British retailing. When he became Chief Executive of Next, the stock market valuation was a mere £25 million and the company was struggling to survive. 16 years later, the company is thriving with a value of £4 billion. David achieved this remarkable turnaround despite privately battling Parkinson's disease.

I first met Derek Arden 15 years ago, shortly after taking over at a struggling NEXT. Derek and I were on different teams in that negotiation, as NEXT attempted to negotiate its banking facilities.

As a result of the way Derek conducted those negotiations both the Bank he represented and NEXT went on to a very profitable and long-term relationship. He was one of only two people in banking that I came across during that difficult time, who had the vision, understanding and skill to negotiate, what he now calls a win/win/win deal.

I heartily recommend this book to anyone that wants to negotiate deals with integrity and for the mutual benefit of all concerned parties. It contains excellent advice that Derek has compiled from 20 years in the field of negotiating.

David Jones CBE.

CONTENTS

"IF YOU ALWAYS DO
WHAT YOU'VE ALWAYS DONE,
YOU WILL ALWAYS GET
WHAT YOU'VE ALWAYS GOT."

CHAPTER 1

YOUR GOALS

- THINK BIG

Most people go through life not actually knowing what they want. When you don't know what you want, you won't get much. Instead of achieving your goals you will be part of someone else's goals, contributing to their success.

One of my favourite quotations comes from Tom Peters, the American Management Consultant, who said -

> *"There are people who make things happen*
> *there are people who watch things happen*
> *and there are people who wonder what happened."*

Which are you?

By buying this book you are now in the first category. Congratulations - stay in this category and make it happen for you.

There is some debate about how many people in the world "make things happen" - it seems like less than 5%.

People who know what they want understand that they have to set goals. These goals should be specific, measurable, outrageous and time-based. If you are familiar with the acronym SMART you will know that it stands for Specific, Measurable, Achievable, Realistic and Time based. The achievable and realistic elements become limiting factors, which put a ceiling on your achievements.

If I had made my goals realistic and achievable, I wouldn't be writing this book for your benefit.

I have been fortunate enough to seek out the very best people in their fields and study them. When I was at the Harvard Business School studying negotiation I learnt of the research that was conducted on their graduating MBA's. They asked the MBA's, how many of them had clear, concise, written down goals; the answer was 3%. These people knew what they wanted, had recorded it on paper and were in pursuit of their targets. 20 years later they tracked down the group and found to everyone's astonishment that the 3%, had 96% of the wealth of the group. If you are happy with an average salary and average responsibility, that's great and you should live your life accordingly.

However if you have an average salary but have more than your fair share of responsibility, then that's not fair and you need to make a change.

If you want to have more income, material wealth and you are prepared to take the responsibility that goes with it; then the sky's the limit. Some people have been brought up to believe that money is the root of all evil, but it is the love of money that is the root of all evil. Money creates options and enables you to be free to do whatever you want to do; to employ people, make charitable donations and help others create wealth.

✸ 60 SECOND TIP
How to know what you want...

All the best thinkers think with a pen in their hand. Ask yourself a high quality question, for example, what do I really want?

Write the question in your journal, notebook or pad. Keep it with you and write down the answers as they come to you.

It may take a while; carry the journal, notebook or pad with you, the answers will come when you least expect them.

You could be asking yourself a question about each of the following seven areas of your life:

1. HEALTH - How can I live a long and healthy life?

Answers might include:
- Exercise three times a week
- Care with your diet (what you eat and drink)
- Mental stimulation
- Financial issues sorted

2. FAMILY- How do I have a long and mutually loving relationship with my close family?

Answers might include:
- Help friends and family achieve their goals
- Sort out all financial issues
- Listen more
- Set time aside for family

3. FINANCE - How can I be financially independent by age 50?

Answers might include:

- X amount of assets
- Mortgage repaid
- Y in pension
- Salary of Z

4. BUSINESS - How can I develop my business interests?

Answers might include:

- Be involved in a separate business as non-executive
- Win new business from a large customer
- Be elected to the Board
- More networking

5. PERSONAL - How can I have some quality time?

Answers might include:

- Schedule some time on my own
- Play some golf
- Read a novel a week
- Leave clear time in my diary for me

6. PERSONAL DEVELOPMENT - How can I grow my knowledge?

Answers might include:

- Invest in three personal development books a year
- Attend seminars, workshops and masterclasses
- Listen to a development CD series in the car
- Meet with people you respect and ask them questions

7. CHARITY - How can I help less fortunate people?

Answers might include:

- Be a trustee on a charity
- Help the local community in a positive way
- Become a school governor
- Set up monthly direct debits for charities

When you have completed this chapter - you will be clearer on your objectives. Often during this process people get a mind block. This is normal, unblock the mind by putting the headings on a pad, having a goal to complete them over a few days, then relax and stop trying..........the answers will come.

Now you know what you want, you can ask what goals you need to set for your job in order to achieve them. Do you need more money? Do you need more time? Do you need more recognition or more opportunities for development?

Most goals have a need for money in the background.
So lets get on and start negotiating your salary.

"YOU ARE PAID TO SERVE. MAKE SURE YOU PROVIDE A GREAT SERVICE FOR YOUR COMPANY AND LOOK AFTER YOUR BOSS."

CHAPTER 2

DOING A GREAT JOB

As long as you are sure that you are in the category of someone who makes it happen, and you are doing a good job, you can move on to the next stage of the book. If you are not, you need to review what you need to do differently, to put you in that category.

Businesses need to make a profit, grow and deliver shareholder value. Your contribution to this is vital and should be measured and rewarded accordingly.

Analyse how you deliver value to the business. Look at how important you are and what the alternatives are if you are not there. Make sure you are pointing out your value, to the right people, at appropriate opportunities.

> *Value is a perception. Perception is reality.*
> *Make sure you are creating the right perception.*

Look at your job description and your job outline. Is that what you actually do? Is it still what the boss wants you to do? What do you do over and above the job description? Re-word and renegotiate the job description to describe what you actually do, pick up the things that you don't do, and question whether you should be doing them. Add things in that you are going to research and do in the future if appropriate. Job descriptions are often muddled up with performance plans. These are separate documents, which should be complementary to each other and will form part of your salary negotiation dossier (SND).

People in responsible jobs have short-term memories, when it comes to results and achievement over the course of the year. Therefore you need to keep diary records of your achievements throughout the year, in your SND.

Diary template - Salary Negotiation Dossier (SND)

DATE	SUCCESS POINT	MONETARY VALUE / ADDED VALUE
28 Feb	Finished project, in time constraints	Presented findings to the committee
16 Mar	New business from major client	£50k
22 May	New client signs contract	£30K

Monetary value is tangible cash flow and profit to the business, in increased sales, increased margins or decreased costs.

Added value is anything that improves the business, but does not have a tangible value. You may have implemented an initiative that improved morale, or reduced the duration of meetings, or streamlined a process.

Ensure you are delivering value to the business. In order to be delivering value in the eyes of the business, you must understand what is important to the business. If your boss tells you that the main priority is to cut costs, talk more about the cutting of costs than quality control or customer satisfaction. It is essential that you are delivering value; that the boss understands, even if you don't agree that it is the most important area to be delivering value in.

Once you are doing this, it will be easier to understand your worth to a business. Wherever possible, you need to record how profitable you are for the business.

Is your knowledge and work really adding value in the following three key areas?

- Order value of your customers
- Number of customers
- Frequency of orders and length of contract/renewals

If you are in the private sector there may be important non-financial criteria eg patient care in National Health Service, compliance with central government, guidelines for local authorities etc.

> *If you can demonstrate that you are adding value in any or all of the three areas above then you have an excellent case for a raise.*

Also, consider these questions which give you good ways to measure your value. What is your relationship with the customers? If you left would the customer follow you?

"FAILING TO PLAN
=
PLANNING TO FAIL."

CHAPTER 3

RESEARCH, RESEARCH & RESEARCH

Benchmark your value to the business.

Having confirmed that you are doing a great job, you can now start to establish how much you are worth to the business. In one model of costing, it costs the company three times the person's salary to employ them (because of the cost of paying national insurance, benefits, computers, training and desk space etc.). What do you think you really cost your employer? How much money do you make for the business? If it is three times your salary, you are only breaking even. If you are making six times your salary then you are adding real value.

Be aware that this is useful information to help you get a good perspective, but is something to be very careful about discussing with your employer. You should only discuss it if it is to your advantage.

Benchmark your value in other industries.

Peer group - who are your peer group? What are they earning and achieving? How do you compare?

Use Internet search engines and go to salary surveys, particularly in the financial press. If you compare the leisure industry with the financial services industry, the financial services industry is much better paid. If you are in a marketing or sales role, then you can work in a variety of industry sectors and you could benchmark the best paid.

You can gather information on salaries from job advertisements, talking to headhunters and you can buy salary surveys for most industries.

Situation analysis

It is essential for your credibility that you ask for a pay rise that is achievable in the current climate. Businesses need to pay people on results. Understand in detail how the economy, your market, your company, your department and your team are doing in comparison to others and in comparison to previous years.

Also look for exceptional events. For example, your company may have had a good year, but if they have just moved to bigger offices, then they may have taken on debt to fund it. This is not your problem! But the management may try to use it against your arguments for a salary increase. So have your arguments well prepared. The offices are a long-term infrastructure investment and should not be unduly affecting the business' day-to-day activities.

Replacement cost of you

What would it cost the business if you left?

These costs can be considerable. Reminding your boss in a non-threatening way of the consequences of you leaving will give more leverage.

Costs might be:-

- Need for temporary cover
- Would they have to offer your replacement a higher salary?
- Loss of new business
- Proper customer service
- Cost of recruitment
    Executive search, headhunters etc.
    Advertisement
    Interview time
    Agency fees
- Training time

"INFORMATION IS POWER -
ONLY
- IF YOU USE IT TO TAKE ACTION."

HARVEY MACKAY

CHAPTER 4

ACTION
- ACTION UNLOCKS WHAT IS ON OFFER

Networking

Build your network, keep in touch with people you know. Make new contacts and show interest in people. Networks will find you new jobs both inside and outside organisations. Winners are always networking. Often people only start networking when they need help and it comes across as so transparent to the people they contact, which leads to poor results.

Profile building and positioning

Writing articles for industry journals will raise your profile AND show you to be a specialist. These are not as difficult to do as most people imagine and can be really successful. Think of the kudos it will bring to your company as well. Journalists can be a great source of contacts and leads. Look for opportunities to write letters to the editor of business magazines etc.

Politics and "playing the game"

Often people say they hate office politics. Most people do, the trouble is people who are good at it often succeed at the expense of others. Human nature likes to criticise the organisation. However criticism of organisations, has a way of coming back to haunt you.

CASE STUDY

Tony worked in a large organisation. He was 55 and had seen change many times. New bosses coming in, changing what other people had done, going back to old ways, re-inventing the wheel etc. He would always say in these circumstances "that's a good idea lets try it". Tony knew you couldn't influence people if you got their backs up. You initially had to go with the flow. Then you could make gentle suggestions that would be much more likely to be accepted. He watched his peer group leave, be made redundant etc. Tony retired at 60 with glowing comments on how helpful he had been to all the management. He had met his goals, earned more money than he had expected and had a quiet grin on his face!

Remember to keep your goals at the front of your mind and keep striving for them. Don't just go with the flow, if this is not taking you towards what you want.

Looking after the boss, and his boss

The boss is the boss. She needs the support of everyone. Sometimes she makes wrong decisions, hopefully most of the time she is right. She makes the decisions on, promotions, bonuses, pay rises etc. So be seen to be supportive to her and her superiors.

Dress for success

Money spent on how you look will pay enormous dividends. The general rule is to dress two jobs above where you are now (unless you are in the military). People will unconsciously notice this and remember when discussions come up for promotion, bonuses etc. that you look and feel ready for promotion.

Set up learning groups

Show your leadership and people skills. What about an ideas committee, to look at ways of improving efficiency? Or a learning group to share specific skills?

Mastermind groups

A mastermind group is a committee of the very best people you know. The group meets regularly to discuss each other's goals and help each other develop.

Mentoring

Set up mentoring groups. Mentor some of the new people and get your own mentor higher up the company or externally.

Build your confidence

This will happen when you take action on the points above. You will be popular, you will be sought after and people will seek out your advice.

Write progress reports, position papers, circulate them to your boss, your boss' boss (with his permission). Ask for advice, ask them to attend groups you set up, ask them for small development budgets, and show them calculations of the extra benefit the company is getting. Get them to introduce the programmes and offer to write their introductions etc.

"IF YOU DON'T ASK - YOU DO NOT GIVE THEM THE OPPORTUNITY TO SAY YES."

CHAPTER 5

ASK FOR IT

Preparation

> "*Proper preparation prevents pretty poor results*"

Most failures are caused by a lack of preparation. One definition of luck is "Where preparation meets opportunity". The opportunity to ask may come when you least expect it. It may not be a one off process because you may have to soften your boss up, to be appreciated that you are very valuable.

"The more I practice the luckier I get", a now famous quote by Gary Player (at one time the best golfer in the world) was heard when he splashed out of a bunker straight into the hole. Practice makes perfect.

Timing

Pick your timing. Present your amended Salary Negotiation Dossier (SND) perhaps called for tactical reasons "a position report" well before any pay date, review or performance appraisal.

Make it look just like a normal progress report, early year-end review or information document. If you do it for example at the end of November, take the opportunity to make realistic forecasts for what you will achieve in December.

Three things to do when asking for a rise:

1. Rehearse
2. Make notes that build your case
3. Control the agenda - as much as you are able.

Softening up

Before you come to the formality of asking, you must consider the softening up process. Softening up is a gambit employed by many people, more notably by politicians publicly, to sway public opinion. For example you might hear "There are going to have to be tax rises at some stage to pay for the increased spending in hospitals." When the tax rises come we are expecting them.

Whenever you are softening up, use the word, "because".

"I am going to have to find a way to increase my pay because.......

        "...the mortgage payments are tough"
        "...my partner wants to move house"
        "...I need to reduce my credit card payments"
        "...I have a goal to repay my student loans by.......

The "because" is very important. Robert Cialdini reports in his book "Influence, Science and Practice", when people made a request for action from other people they had a 30% increase in their success rate by adding the word "because" to their request. It was not the reason that swayed the situation it was the use of the word "because".
The "because" adds credibility and authority to the statement.

At the review

All reviews will have their own procedure. You must respect this as trying to buck it will only put the boss's back up and reduce the chances of you negotiating the package you want. Wait until the boss has gone through the company procedure and then perhaps say, "I would like to present some additional information that I would like you to be aware of..."

Opening position

Ask for a high opening specific number which is your best position (BP) (see chapter 8). Make it high, however you might qualify it with "around".

> *"I am looking for around £50,000" (when you are looking for £45,000). Around means you have flagged that they don't have to offer you quite £50,000.*

If you have worked 300 hours overtime (because of the amount of work you contribute, not because you are slow) with an hourly cost rate of £20, then you might consider asking for an increase of up to £6000. Beware of basing your argument for an increase on hours worked rather than value delivered, as the boss may just decide you are an inefficient worker.

If you can demonstrate that you have delivered more projects on time than average staff, or made more money or delivered more sales then you have a stronger case for your increase.

If you've done your homework, you are unlikely to get a no. You are more likely to get a "thank you; we'll get back to you."

Be careful with deadlines because they can force decisions from people that you may not want. The negotiation process for what you want could be a long one and you may not be able to achieve your goals at the first review.

"WHEN YOU CAN'T GET A PAY RISE, WHAT CAN YOU GET?"

CHAPTER 6

NEGOTIABLE VARIABLES

- THE SMALL THINGS THAT MAKE A BIG DIFFERENCE

Negotiable variables are the items that can be of particular value to one of the parties but do not cost the other party so much. They can include all sorts of things depending on your industry.

Make a list of the items that may be relevant in your industry. On the next page are a selection of the type of benefits to which I am referring.

Often these can sometimes be easier for people to agree. Many of them are also win/win situations making both sides feel good.

Sometimes these benefits come out of different budgets from the salaries, enabling the benefits to be hidden in the remuneration structure.

Bonus or commission
on any new income you create for the company

- Employers love the opportunity to pay you on results.

Share options

- This shows you are committed to the long term success of the business.
- You can ask for shadow options if the company is not quoted.

Car

- You may want a company car -You may want a better model.
- You may want to reduce your petrol costs, so ask for a diesel.

Petrol

- The company may have a local account that you can become a signatory on occasionally.
- The company may be prepared to pay all your petrol costs. (Take care regarding your tax position).

Insurance

- The company may be able to get a better price on health insurances if they include more people.

Mobile phone

- Use of a company phone may save you money, but because business tariffs are cheaper, might not be a major cost to the company.
- Business line at home.

New technology

- The people who had laptops first were able to work smarter and more efficiently, and in many cases from home. Technology is now very cost-effective and the technology may be tax deductible for the company. There may be another benefit in the ability to work from home.

Clothes allowance

- If looking smart is key to your role, but it is costing you a great deal of money, ask for an allowance. Make it clear that you are asking because you care about your appearance and how it reflects favourably on the business.

Accommodation allowance

- If you work for a multinational organisation that offers accommodation allowances for people living abroad there may be a budget that you can access when the payroll hasn't got any space to give an increase.
- If you stay away on business - you could negotiate an increased hotel allowance.

A new title

- Your colleagues may rib you for just negotiating a better title such as 'relationship director' rather than 'relationship manager' but there are many hidden benefits. Clients will treat you differently and you will be able to win more orders or complete more projects as a result. Also, if you decide to leave the company, your CV will show that you have been promoted.

Training or study leave

- If there are skills you need, then get the company to pay for it.
- Study leave, for qualifications you are prepared to pay for.
- Companies often pay for MBA's or postgraduate courses. But be careful you may have to sign a contract to pay the money back if you leave within a specified time. The company may also consider it as "golden handcuffs" and decide not to give you a pay rise.
- A day on an interpersonal skills workshop - such as a negotiation skills masterclass.....

Client entertainment allowance - to include your partner

- Entertaining your clients will help you grow your relationship for both your future career and the business. By being able to take your partner, you may not be compromising your home life as much by working late or unsociable hours.
- Entertaining clients at home
- Two season tickets at your local football team for client entertainment

Flexible working hours

- If your goals tell you that you need more time out of the office, at home, on the golf course or wherever, why not ask for flexibility about when and where you work?
- Agreement to working 8 hours between 8am and 8pm
- Agreement to any 40 hours per week
- Agreement to 1950 hours in any year
- 4 days a week - but 35 hours

Additional holidays

- If they can't give you more money they can always give you more time. Before asking for this, work out the marginal cost of each additional day to the company so that you can make a case for it if you need to.

Opportunities to speak at conferences

- If this will help you build profile in order to achieve your long term career goals, but it costs the company nothing then why not ask for this?

Child care facilities

- Crèche at work
- The company pays for the crèche
- The company pays partly for crèche facilities
- On call nurse

Party

- By getting management to agree that your team can have their own end of year party or a party for meeting a target, you will be appreciated by your team and should be able to get more out of them.

"IT IS 5 TIMES MORE DIFFICULT TO LIE WITH BODY LANGUAGE THAN IT IS WITH WORDS."

DR DAVID LEWIS. PSYCHOLOGIST

CHAPTER 7

ESSENTIAL INTERPERSONAL SKILLS

Questioning

A question is the most powerful thing you can use to gather information. A high quality question is something you have thought through in advance, aimed at gathering information, seeing where the other person is coming from so that you can prepare your case.

Asking good quality questions around the organisation will help the benchmarking process in that people will give you information, point you in the direction of finding information and will also often tell you things that you didn't expect to hear.

Be careful about gossip - check other people's agendas and don't use 'grapevine' information without checking thoroughly. If people ask you personal questions about other individuals, be neutral in your response no matter what you think about them.

Listening

Don't just ask the questions, actively listen to the answers!

Listening requires discipline and concentration. We have two ears and two eyes to listen with and we should use them all the time to pick up on any subtle clue that might help us. Ask open questions and resist the temptation to qualify them. See what the other person says first. Their interpretation of your question as much as their response will give you valuable information.

Listen to the voice tonality and any clues. Listen and look for what is not said.

Body Language

Non-verbal clues will be given in body language. It is 5 times more difficult to lie with body language than it is with words. Observe carefully and interpret in the wide context.

If you are unsure about your boss's response ask a closed question and listen carefully to the answer. e.g. "Will you put my case to the directors as I have presented it?".

Creativity

The ability to brainstorm the issues, use creative right brain thinking techniques to analyse how you are going to achieve your goals, is important.

Get a book or a mentor to help you with this if you are not sure how to start.

A very practical method is to take an A4 sheet of paper and write the question you want answered at the very top of the page. (it is important you actually write a question mark after the question)

Then write as quickly as you can all the answers that come into your head. Keep going until you have a minimum of 15 answers. Then evaluate the answers to find the ones that are useful for the circumstances.

"SOMETIMES YOU HAVE TO USE A PLOY TO GET THE OTHER PERSON TO SEE WHERE YOU ARE COMING FROM."

CHAPTER 8

PLOYS, GAMBITS & TACTICS

Ploys, gambits and tactics help to make your position clear to the other person or perhaps change their perception of where the power lies.

> *We all know that no one is bigger than the organisation; however that doesn't mean the organisation can abuse you in what they pay you.*

When all else fails, sometimes you have to make people listen to what you are saying. Sometimes you have to demonstrate you are serious about your goals. You may need to change your job. However, you may have worked in a company for a long time and be locked into a long-term pension where you don't feel you have a walk away position (WAP). You always have options. But sometimes they don't seem very sensible until you have help with them.

Best position, Target position, Walk away position and Alternative position form your four value strategies to get what you want:

BP - *your dream position* - you never know they may agree

TP - *reasonable position* - your target

WAP - where you cannot go any lower

AP - What your alternatives are if you can't get agreement. What you will do and what opportunities will open up if you have to go this route. e.g. Leave, join a competitor, retrain, re-skill…

Analyse these carefully in your plan, however be prepared to change these (upwards or downwards) depending on what information comes to hand.

Separate the people from the problem

Negotiation issues are problems that can be resolved. Make them opportunities by outside the box thinking. Keep them separated from the individuals. Use phrases like

"I understand your situation, and it's nothing personal. However I need to be paid more for the value I create, because I have a family to support." Use the because word and an empathetic statement to support it.

Make yourself indispensable

Have knowledge, go to meetings, conferences, look after the boss, be privy to privileged information, and be supportive in difficult times.

Be a confidant, mentor, key person, be a friend to wives, family members and a thoroughly nice person. Do this sincerely for the right reasons and NOT just for your goals. If you are insincere you will be seen through immediately in the way you behave.

Trade concessions

You are unlikely to get everything you want. Decide in the planning stage the really key issues and the items that don't matter. This gives you control when it comes to bargaining. You know what you are happy to give up, to enable you to get what you really want.

Any quality negotiator will have must haves and nice to haves prepared and be ready to trade nice to haves for must haves.

The key language to use is, "If you will agree to £X,000 per year then I will withdraw my request for permanent health insurance" - one is conditional on the other.

Act in anger, don't react in anger

One tactic you can use in this situation is to 'throw your toys out of the pram.' If you are certain you have due cause, then you may need to express your discontent clearly and passionately. It can sometimes be effective to do this by email, because this gives the other person time to digest the information and take on board how serious you are.

Grapevine

Another tactic is to start a rumour, however you need to be very careful. For example, tell someone over a drink who is close to the boss's PA that you have been offered another job worth more money, but you'd rather stay if you can. Be cautious with the rumour tactic as it can backfire. Chinese whispers could turn such a comment into 'MATTHEW is planning to leave…' Don't do this unless you are and you are working on your alternative position. Not a tactic I would recommend except in exceptional circumstances.

"Is that it? Is that all I am worth?"

Another tactic is when you get a pay rise or bonus; you ask a question, such as "Is that it, is that all I am worth?", in a very disappointed tone. Careful with this tactic as it can only be used sparingly.

Alternative position crystallised

When you get an alternative job offer, try to get it in writing. This will put you in the strongest position to be able to negotiate with your existing employer. Again consider softening your boss up, talking to them at the right time in the right place (set this up) and saying something along the lines of, "I have had this job offer, I don't know what to do. I like our company, I enjoy working here however income and job prospects are very important to me (and my family). Is there anything you can do for me?"

If a head-hunter is involved, they may try and get to you to feel committed to the other company and themselves by using closing tactics on you before they put it in writing. Be careful of this.

All of the above needs to be handled thoughtfully, carefully and at just the right time. It can be quite stressful which is why having a knowledgeable friend or business coach can be extremely helpful in these situations.

CASE STUDY

I often coach people in these situations, let me tell you about Matt. Matt had been working for a company for thirty years. He was not being paid his value and the company had assumed he was 'a lifer' and didn't need to be incentivised further. He was offered a £1,000 pay rise. I had coached Matt to say that he realised his direct boss was not responsible and that he was very happy with their personal relationship, but that he was shocked and hurt. Matt explained that after all the deals he did the year before and the long hours and the weekends he'd worked he knew he was worth more to the business than his present package. I had suggested to Matt to go home for the day as he was so shocked.

Matt returned to the office on Monday and his boss wasn't speaking to him. So I advised Matt to go in and repeat that he had no problem with his boss, he knew it wasn't down to him but he was still shocked and hurt. A week later his boss arranged for him to have a substantial pay rise.

Get yourself a coach or a genuine confidant who won't start a rumour.

If your employer doesn't want to negotiate and nor do you -
What are the alternatives?

If you get a "no", no matter how resolute the "no" seemed, most employers will feel some element of guilt. They will not think less of you for asking for more money. Indeed, they should be pleased that you have asked, because they will then know that when representing the business you won't be afraid to ask appropriately for more business, higher pricing etc.

> *Get back to work and continue to work long hours*
> *- but only in areas that will be valued by the boss.*

Ask for the criteria to meet in order to get your pay rise and then ask for regular reviews to ensure you are on course. Ask that the pay rise be given when the targets are met, not when the next review comes up. People do what they are measured on, make sure you are doing that or negotiate a change in the measurements.

> *Ask the boss to give you a long-term career path.*
> *What are the opportunities for development and*
> *growth within the company?*

Will the company help place you in another department or business in order to keep you motivated for the next 12 - 24 months whilst the current project is delivered?

*CAREFULLY CONSTRUCTED PHRASES THAT
CAN WORK...*

- *What can you do for me?*
- *Can you do something for me?*
- *Can you help me here?*
- *I was hoping the organisation could do more than that for me!*
- *That wasn't the number I had in mind!*
- *I am not sure that recognises my value!*
- *My wife / husband / partner will be very disappointed!*
- *That doesn't take me to where I need to be*

Add your own phrases - check they are soft and not aggressive.

"IT HAS BEEN MY OBSERVATION THAT MOST PEOPLE GET AHEAD DURING THE TIME THAT OTHERS WASTE."

HENRY FORD

SUMMARY

The key steps you need to go through:

- Preparation
- Planning
- Research
- Asking high quality questions
- Listening with all your body
- Networking
- Using tactics and creativity
- Bargaining with confidence

This book is designed to achieve more success for you in the important area of understanding people.

You can apply the principles to other types of negotiations.

Dip in and out of it, carry it in your pocket and offer it to other people. Monitor how you understand people better and notice your better relationships.

If you always do
What you have always done
You will always get
What you have always got

Try something different, if it doesn't work try something else.
You can always go back to what you did before

SALARY NEGOTIATION DOSSIER

DATE	SUCCESS POINT	MONETARY VALUE / ADDED VALUE

SELF COACHING QUESTIONS

Why do I want a pay rise?

On a scale of 1 -100 - how important is it to me?

What are the most important goals, on my goal sheet?

What are my negotiable variables?

What is stopping me asking for a raise?

Where can I talk to my boss, when he will be receptive to listening?

What tactics may I have to use?

Who is the best person to approach?

From whom can I gather information?

Is the hassle worth it? (ANSWER YES!)

NOTE PAD

Other products by Derek Arden

Derek Arden is a prolific Speaker, Author and Business Coach. For more of his learning aids, books and audio products visit

www.derekarden.co.uk
email: derek@derekarden.co.uk

Derek Arden International Limited
Tiptree House Publishing
PO Box 974
Guildford
Surrey
United Kingdom
GU19BR

00 44 (0) 1483 505854 (office)
00 44 (0) 1483 532880 (fax)
00 44 (0) 7980 241185 (direct)